Padua
Italy

City Map

 Glob:us

Padua, Italy — City Map
By Jason Patrick Bates

First Edition: February 2017

Scale / 1:4000

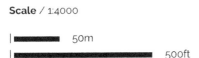

50m

500ft

Map Overview

Map Symbols

Highway		Map continuation page	
Street		Path	

Archaeological site		Kiosk	
Artwork		Level crossing	
Atm		Library	
Bar		Lighthouse	
Bicycle rental		Memorial	
Biergarten		Memorial plaque	
Buddhist temple		Monument	
Bus station		Museum	
Bus stop		Muslim mosque	
Cafe		Neighbourhood	
Camping site		Nightclub	
Car rental		Parking	
Cave entrance		Peak	
Chalet		Pharmacy	
Charging station		Picnic site	
Church / Monastery		Playground	
Cinema		Police	
Courthouse		Post office	
Department store		Prison	
Dog park		Pub	
Drinking water		Railway	
Dry cleaning		Restaurant	
Elevator		Shinto temple	
Embassy		Sikh temple	
Fast food		Sports centre	
Ferry terminal		Supermarket	
Fire station		Taoist temple	
Fountain		Taxi	
Fuel		Telephone	
Golf course		Theatre	
Guest house		Toilets	
Hindu temple		Townhall	
Hospital		Traffic signals	
Hostel		Viewpoint	
Hotel		Water park	
Information		Wilderness hut	
Jewish synagogue		Windmill	

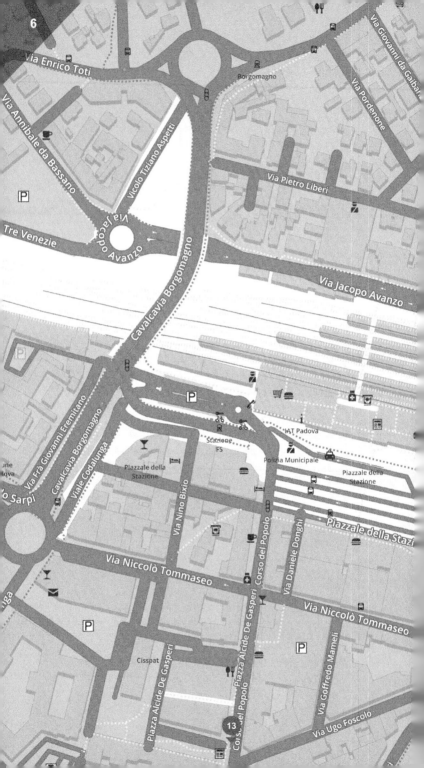

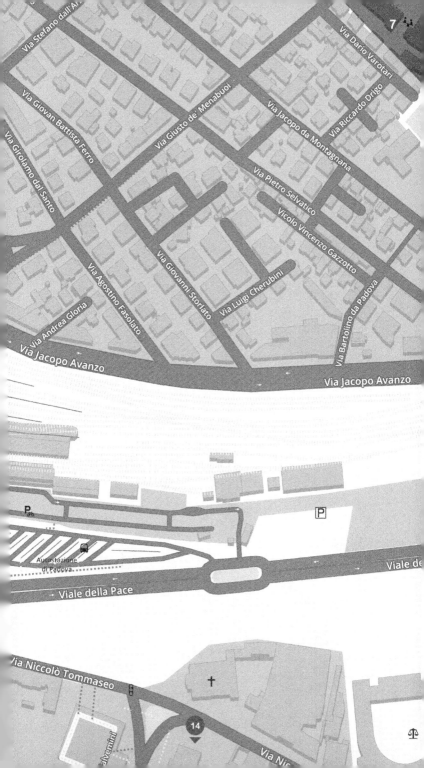

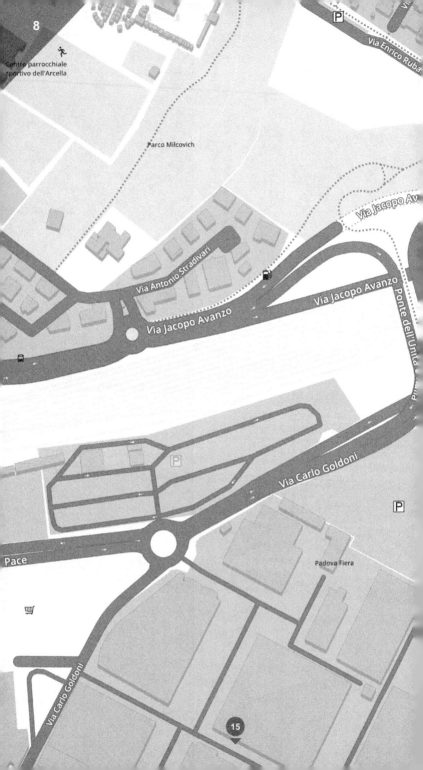

5

Vicolo della Bovetta

Viale Codalunga

Palazzo Maldura

Via del Carmine

Passeggiata del Carmine

Passeggiata del Carmine

Via Caltura

Via Montona

Piazzetta
Beato Giordano
Forzaté

Via dei Savonarola

Via Antonio Tolomei

Riviera dei Mugnai

Riv

Via San Pietro

Via San Fermo

Via San Polo

Via dei Borromeo

Via Calatafimi

Via Rolando da Piazzola

Via Sant'Agnese

Via Dante

Leoni

Vicolo dei Dotto

Piazza Insurrezio

Milano

INPS

P

Teatro Giuseppe
Verdi

Via San Nicolò

Via Giuseppe Verdi

Dondi Dall'Orologio

Da Carrara

Via Dante

20

Via Belle Parti

Via Aquileia

Oratorio
San Rocco

Via Santa Lucia

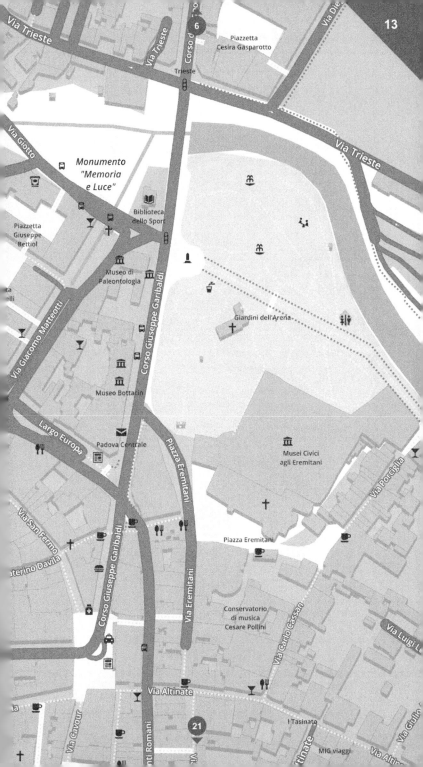

Via Trieste

Via Trieste

Corso d'...

6

Piazzetta
Cesira Gasparotto

Via Die...

Via Trieste

Trieste

Via Giotto

Monumento
"Memoria
e Luce"

Piazzetta
Giuseppe
Bettiol

Biblioteca
dello Sport

Museo di
Paleontologia

Corso Giuseppe Garibaldi

Giardini dell'Arena

Via Giacomo Matteotti

Museo Bottacin

Largo Europa

Padova Centrale

Piazza Eremitani

Musei Civici
agli Eremitani

Via Porciglia

Via San Fermo

aterino Davila

Piazza Eremitani

Via Eremitani

Conservatorio
di musica
Cesare Pollini

Via Carlo Cassan

Via Luigi L...

Via Cavour

Via Altinate

21

I Tasinato

MIG viaggi

Via Alti...

Via Giulio...

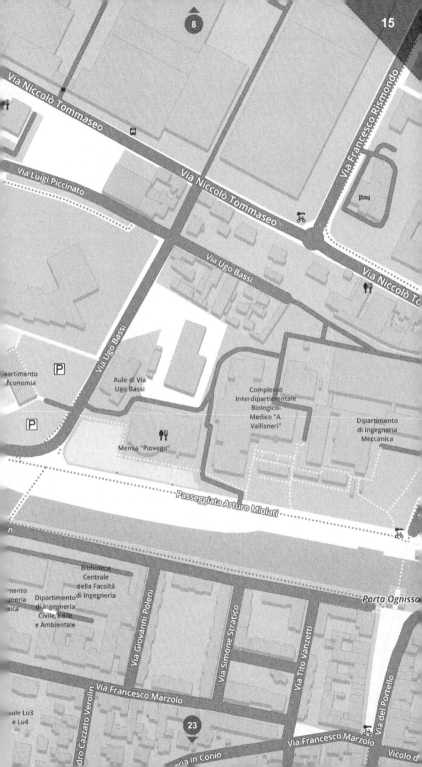

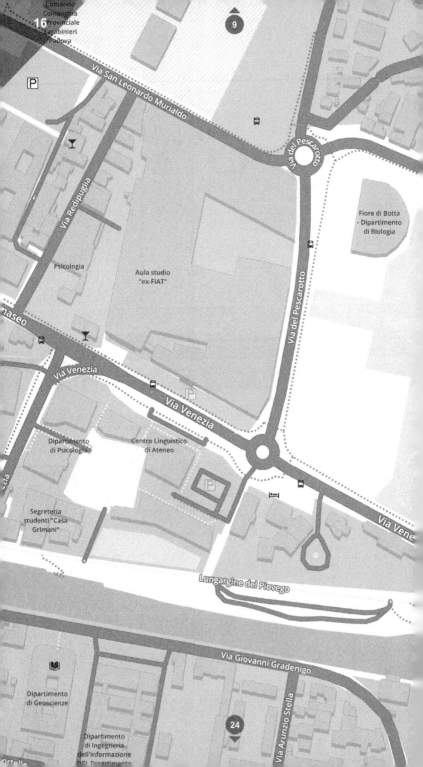

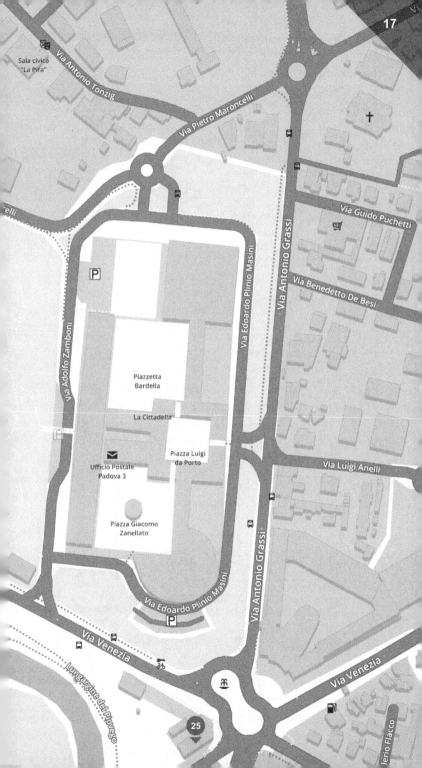

Sala civica "La Pira"

Via Antonio Tonzig

Via Pietro Maroncelli

elli

Via Guido Puchetti

Via Adolfo Zamboni

Via Edoardo Plinio Masini

Via Antonio Grassi

Via Benedetto De Besi

P

Piazzetta Bardella

La Cittadella

Piazza Luigi da Porto

Ufficio Postale Padova 3

Via Luigi Anelli

Piazza Giacomo Zanellato

Via Antonio Grassi

Via Edoardo Plinio Masini

P

Via Venezia

Via Venezia

Lungargine del Piovego

25

lerio Flacco

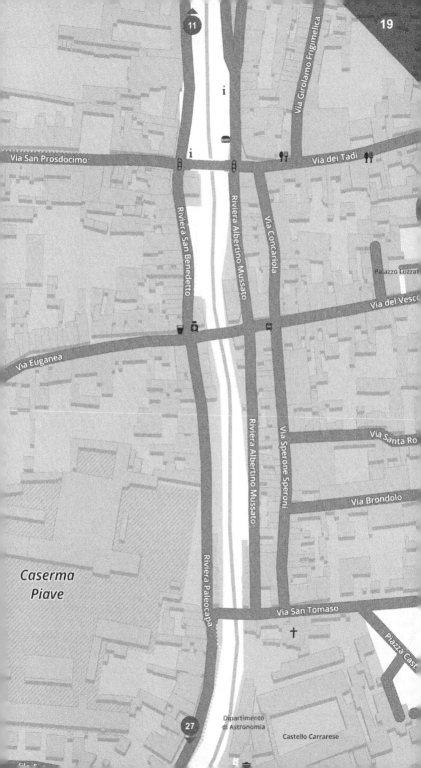

affè Pedrocchi

Via VIII Febbraio

Ponti Romani

Via Cesare Battisti

Palazzo del Bo

Via San Biagio

Via Cesare Battisti

Via degli Zabarella

Via Fabio Filzi

Via San Francesco

Via -

lleria Storione

Piazza Antenore

Prefettura di Padova

Via San Francesco

Vicolo Santa Margherita

Via del Santo

Museo di Storia della Medicina in Padova

Via Santa Sofia

Riviera Tito Livio

ESU

Via Gaspara Stampa

Via Su

zante

medale neo

Via Galileo Galilei

Via Santa Chiara

ra

Via Rudena

Via del Santo

29

dena

Via Bartolor

13

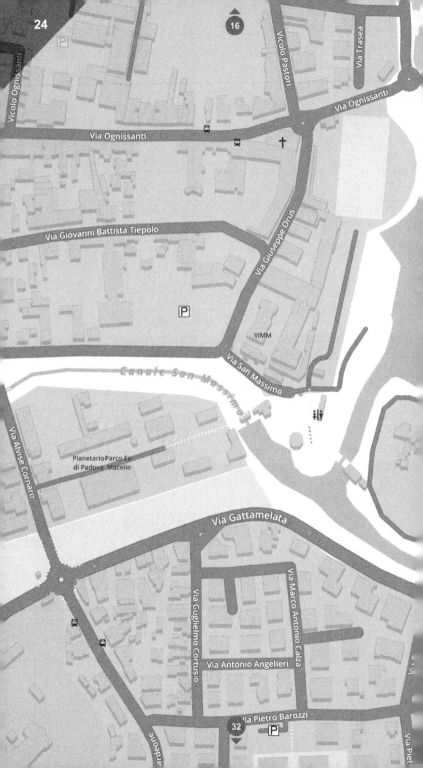

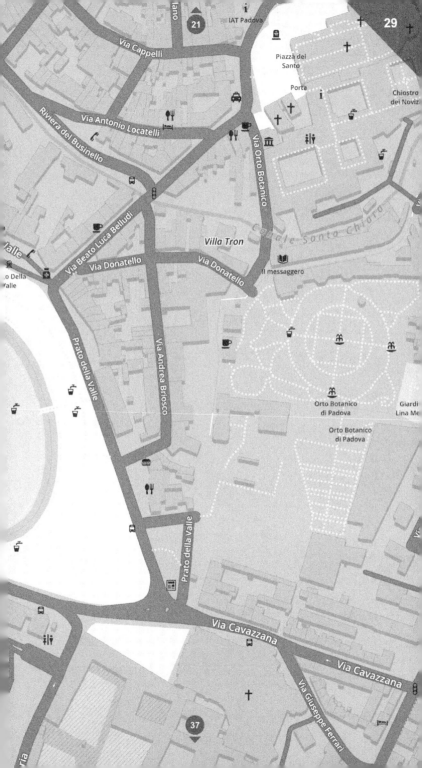

IAT Padova

Piazza del Santo

Porta

Chiostro dei Noviz

Via Cappelli

Via Antonio Locatelli

Riviera del Businello

Via Orto Botanico

Via Beato Luca Belludi

Villa Tron

Canale Santa Chiara

Via Donatello

Via Donatello

Il messaggero

o Della Valle

alle

Prato della Valle

Via Andrea Briosco

Orto Botanico di Padova

Giardi Lina Me

Orto Botanico di Padova

Prato della Valle

Via Cavazzana

Via Cavazzana

Via Giuseppe Ferrari

22

Vicolo Santonini

Via Bartolomeo D'Aviano

Via Pietro Scalcerle

Via Gustavo Mode

Porta Pontecorvo

Via Vittoria Aganoor

Via Jacopo Facciolati

Via Alessandro Manzoni

Via Michele Sanmicheli

Via Alessandro Stoppato

Via Cesare Pollini

Via Alessandro Manzoni

Via Lazzaro Bonamico

Via Luigi Bottazzo

Via Leopoldo Ferri

Via Giuseppe Veronese

Via Pi

38

Raimondo Diaz

Corso Vittorio Em

Via Alberto Mario

28

Via Giosuè Carducci

Via Gi

Velodromo
Giovanni
Monti

Via Edmondo De Amicis

Stadio Silvio
Appiani

Via Giovanni Malaman

Via Giosuè Carducci

Via Marghera

Via Giordano Bru

Vicc

Via Giordano Bruno

Via delle Rose

Andrea Costa

Via Tre Garofani

Leonardo Emo-Capodilista

Via Guglielmino Tempesta

Via dei Pioppi

Via Barroccio Dal

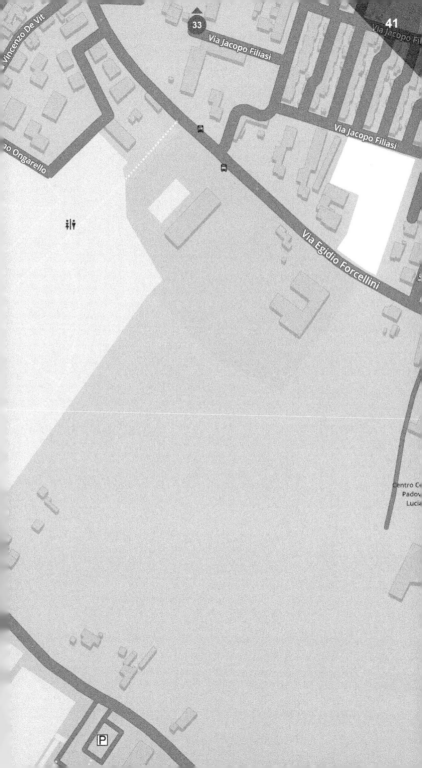

Streets

B

Barriera saracinesca . 26, 27

C

Cavalcavia borgo-
  magno 6
Cavalcavia dalmazia 4, 5
Corso del popolo . . 6, 13
Corso delle tre venezie
  5, 6
Corso giuseppe
  garibaldi 13
Corso milano 10–12
Corso vittorio emanuele
  ii 28, 36
Corte arco valaresso . 20

G

Galleria alcide de
  gasperi 6
Galleria brancaleone . 13
Galleria calatafimi 12
Galleria degli scrovegni
  14
Galleria degli zabarella
  13
Galleria dei borromeo 12
Galleria delle porte
  contarine 13
Galleria duomo 20
Galleria eremitani 13
Galleria europa 13
Galleria ezzelino 12
Galleria fratelli ruffini . 14
Galleria giovanni
  berchet 14
Galleria giuseppe
  garibaldi 13

Galleria milano 11
Galleria ognissanti . . . 23
Galleria san bernardino
  21
Galleria santa lucia 13, 21
Galleria storione 21
Galleria tito livio . . 20, 21
Galleria trieste 14

L

Largo egidio
  meneghetti 14
Largo europa 13
Lungargine del piovego
  15–17, 24, 25

P

Passaggio elena lu-
  crezia corner pis-
  copia 12
Passaggio gaspare
  gozzi 14
Passaggio luigi gauden-
  zio 13
Passaggio san fermo . 12
Passaggio san nicolò . 12
Passaggio tito livio . . . 21
Passeggiata arturo mio-
  lati 14,
  15
Passeggiata bianchini
  d'alberigo giulia . 31,
  32, 40
Passeggiata conciapelli
  12
Passeggiata del
  carmine 12
Passeggiata f. cammil-
  lotti 27,
  35

Passeggiata lazzari
  maria 40
Piazza accademia delia
  27
Piazza alcide de gasperi
  6
Piazza antenore 21
Piazza capitaniato 20
Piazza castello . . . 19, 20
Piazza cavour 13, 21
Piazza de gasperi 6
Piazza dei frutti 20
Piazza dei signori 20
Piazza del duomo 20
Piazza del santo . . 21, 29
Piazza dell'insurrezione
  28 aprile 1945 . . . 12
Piazza delle erbe 20
Piazza eremitani 13
Piazza francesco pe-
  trarca 12
Piazza gaetano salvem-
  ini 7,
  14
Piazza garibaldi 13
Piazza giacomo zanel-
  lato 17
Piazza giuseppe
  garibaldi 13
Piazza insurrezione . . . 12
Piazza luigi da porto . . 17
Piazza napoli 34, 35
Piazza petrarca 12
Piazza salvemini . . . 7, 14
Piazza turati 14
Piazzale della stazione 7
Piazzale di porta
  savonarola . . . 10, 11
Piazzale di porta trento
  3, 4
Piazzale firenze 26
Piazzale giuseppe
  mazzini 12

Piazzale mazzini 5
Piazzale pontecorvo . 30
Piazzale san giovanni 18
Piazzale san giuseppe
   18
Piazzale santa croce . 36
Piazzale stanga 17
Piazzale stazione 6
Piazzetta amedeo sar-
   tori 12,
   13
Piazzetta bardella 17
Piazzetta beato gior-
   dano forzate 12
Piazzetta cappellato
   pedrocchi 21
Piazzetta cesira gas-
   parotto 13
Piazzetta colonna 22
Piazzetta conciapelli . 13
Piazzetta della garzeria
   21
Piazzetta francesco
   canova 28
Piazzetta giovanni
   palatucci 20, 21
Piazzetta girotto mari-
   ano 21
Piazzetta giuseppe bet-
   tiol 13
Piazzetta giuseppe bus-
   solin 12,
   13
Piazzetta lucia valentini
   terrani 12
Piazzetta padre massi-
   miliano kolbe . . . 29
Piazzetta san michele 27
Piazzetta san nicolò . . 12
Piazzetta turati 14
Pilade bronzetti 10
Ponte antonio milani . 13,
   14
Ponte balbino del nun-
   zio 15
Ponte conciapelli 12
Ponte corvo 22, 30
Ponte dell'unità d'italia
   8, 9
Ponte di ferro 11
Ponte goito 35
Ponte paleocapa 27
Ponte san giovanni
   delle navi 19
Ponte san gregorio bar-
   barigo 20
Ponte san lorenzo . 12, 21

Ponte sant'agostino . . 19
Ponte silvio omizzolo . 14
Prato della valle . . 28, 29

R

Riviera albertino mus-
   sato 11, 12,
   19
Riviera dei mugnai 12, 13
Riviera dei ponti romani
   13, 21
Riviera del businello . 29
Riviera paleocapa 19, 26,
   27
Riviera ruzante . . . 20, 21,
   28, 29
Riviera san benedetto 11,
   19
Riviera tiso camposan-
   piero 20,
   27
Riviera tito livio . . . 20, 21
Rondò borgomagno . . 6

S

Selciato san nicolò . . . 12

V

Via 20 settembre 20
Via 4 novembre . . 27, 28,
   36
Via accademia 20
Via achille de giovanni
   39, 40
Via acquette 28
Via adolfo zamboni . . . 17
Via agostino fasolato . . 7
Via agostino palesa . 30,
   31
Via agrigento 34
Via al municipio 20
Via albania 35
Via alberto cavalletto 27,
   28
Via alberto da baone 36
Via alberto da osa 37
Via alberto da padova 11
Via alberto de mandelo
   36
Via alberto mario 36
Via aleardo aleardi . . 20,
   27, 28
Via alessandria 26

Via alessandro cazzato
   verolin 15, 23
Via alessandro decalzi
   31
Via alessandro knips
   macoppe 38
Via alessandro manzoni
   30, 37, 38
Via alessandro poerio 3,
   11
Via alessandro pros-
   docimi 33
Via alessandro stoppato
   30
Via alfredo catalani . 8, 9
Via alicorno 35
Via altichieri da zevio . . 9
Via altinate 13, 21, 22
Via alvise cornaro . 23, 24
Via amerigo vespucci 35
Via amilcare ponchielli 8
Via ancona 26, 34
Via andrea briosco . . . 29
Via andrea costa . 35, 36
Via andrea gloria 7
Via andrea gritti 20
Via andrea mantegna 13
Via andrea memmo . . 28
Via andrea meneghini
   20
Via andrea vesalio 14
Via angelo barzon . . . 35
Via angelo bristot 28
Via angelo messedaglia
   38, 39
Via angelo portenari . . 5
Via angelo riello 27
Via angelo scarsellini 30
Via annibale da bas-
   sano 5,
   6
Via antonio abetti 40
Via antonio angelieri . 24
Via antonio bagatella . 9
Via antonio bajamonti 12,
   13
Via antonio baldissera
   35
Via antonio bonardi . . 33
Via antonio da tempo 25
Via antonio francesco
   bomporti 20
Via antonio gramsci . . . 9
Via antonio grassi 17
Via antonio locatelli . 29
Via antonio meucci . . 40
Via antonio pertile 31, 39

Via antonio piazza . . . 30
Via antonio rosmini . . . 31
Via antonio rossato . . . 32
Via antonio sciesa 9
Via antonio simeone
  sografi 31
Via antonio smareglia . 7
Via antonio stradivari . . 8
Via antonio tolomei . . 12
Via antonio tonzig 17
Via aosta 26
Via aquileia 12
Via arco valaresso . . . 20
Via aristide gabelli . . . 22
Via aristide stefani . . . 40
Via armando diaz . 35, 36
Via armando montini . 27
Via arnaldo fusinato 4, 11
Via arrigo boito 27
Via arunzio stella . 16, 24
Via augusto anfossi . . 17
Via avellino 34
Via azimo degli azimi 36,
  37
Via barroccio dal borgo
  36
Via bartolino da padova
  7
Via bartolomeo bellano
  21, 29
Via bartolomeo colleoni
  33, 41
Via bartolomeo cristo-
  fori 12
Via bartolomeo
  d'aviano 30
Via bartolomeo sig-
  noroni 38
Via beato luca belludi 29
Via beato pellegrino . . 4,
  12
Via beato salvo
  d'acquisto 9
Via belfiore 3, 4
Via belle parti 12
Via benedetto cairoli . . 6
Via benedetto de besi 17
Via benevento 34
Via bengasi 18, 26
Via bergamo 26
Via bernardino
  scardeone . . . 24, 32
Via bernardo gonzati 31,
  32, 39, 40
Via bezzecca 3, 4
Via biagio brugi . . . 37, 38
Via bligny 10

Via boccalerie 12, 20
Via bonaventura da
  peraga 17
Via brigata padova 10, 18
Via brondolo 19, 20
Via cagliari 26
Via calatafimi 12
Via caltura 12
Via camillo manfroni . 37,
  38
Via campagnola . . . 11, 12
Via cappelli 29
Via caprera 10
Via cardinale pietro
  maffi 3
Via carlo cassan 13
Via carlo cerato 28
Via carlo de brosses . 32,
  33
Via carlo dottori 20
Via carlo goldoni 8, 9, 14
Via carlo guido patin . 32
Via carlo leoni 11, 12
Via carlo pisacane 3
Via carlo rezzonico . . . 14
Via carlo tivaroni . 33, 40,
  41
Via carso 10
Via caserta 34
Via castelfidardo 26
Via castelmorrone . 3, 10
Via caterino davila 13
Via cavazzana 29
Via cavour 13
Via cernaia 18, 26
Via cesare battisti . 21, 22
Via cesare pollini 30
Via cesarotti 22
Via cinquantottesimo
  fanteria . . 29, 36, 37
Via citolo da perugia 4, 5
Via claudio monteverdi
  8
Via coatit 10
Via col di lana 18
Via collegio san marco
  11
Via como 34
Via concariola 19
Via concetto marchesi
  30, 38
Via coni zugna 18
Via corrado lubian . . . 18
Via cosenza 26
Via cremona 26
Via cristoforo colombo
  27

Via cristoforo moro . . 18,
  26
Via cuneo 26
Via curtatone e monta-
  nara 18
Via dalmazia 5
Via damiano chiesa . . 22
Via daniele donghi 6
Via daniele manin . . . 20
Via dante 12, 20
Via dardanelli 3
Via dario delù 14
Via dario varotari 7
Via degli agnusdei . . . 22
Via degli obizzi 20
Via degli zabarella 13, 21
Via dei borromeo 12
Via dei cappuccini . . . 35
Via dei da carrara . 12, 20
Via dei dondi
  dall'orologio . 12, 20
Via dei fabbri 20
Via dei gatari 32
Via dei livello 11, 12
Via dei mille 18, 26
Via dei papafava 20
Via dei pioppi 36
Via dei rogati 20
Via dei savonarola 10–12
Via dei soncin 20
Via dei tadi 19, 20
Via del carmine . . 12, 13
Via del municipio . 20, 21
Via del padovanino . . . 21
Via del pescarotto . 9, 16
Via del portello . . . 15, 23
Via del risorgimento . 12,
  13
Via del santo 21, 29
Via del seminario . 20, 28
Via del torresino . . 27, 28
Via del vescovado 19, 20
Via dell'arco 16, 20
Via della paglia 27
Via della pieve 21, 22
Via delle melette 10
Via delle palme 5
Via delle piazze 20
Via delle porte con-
  tarine 13
Via delle rose 36, 37
Via diego valeri . . 6, 7, 13
Via dietro duomo . 19, 20
Via digione 10
Via dimesse 27, 28
Via domenico bonati . . 7

Via domenico turazza 17,
25
Via domenico vandelli
20
Via don giovanni verità
16, 17
Via donatello 29
Via duca degli abruzzi
27, 35
Via edmondo de amicis
36
Via edoardo bassini . . 39
Via edoardo plinio
masini 17
Via egidio forcellini . . 31–
33, 41
Via emanuele filiberto
di savoia 12, 13
Via emilio teza 31
Via enrico berlinguer . 14
Via enrico catellani . . 40
Via enrico caviglia . . 3, 4
Via enrico de regnier . 32
Via enrico degli
scrovegni 14
Via enrico rubaltelli . 8, 9
Via enrico toti 6
Via eremitani 13
Via ettore romagnoli . 38
Via euganea 18, 19
Via eugenio curiel 9
Via eugenio ruspoli . . . 3
Via ezzelino il balbo . 26,
27
Via fabio filzi 21
Via fabrici girolamo
d'acquapendente
37
Via fabris 32
Via federico con-
falonieri 16,
17
Via federico cordenons
33
Via federico lori 37
Via federico viscidi . . . 37
Via ferdinando coletti 15
Via fistomba 17, 25
Via fiume 20
Via flavio busonera . . . 12
Via fra' paolo sarpi 4
Via francesco agusto
bon 31
Via francesco baracca
10
Via francesco beltrami
10

Via francesco bonafede
39
Via francesco bonatelli
39
Via francesco corradini
40
Via francesco
dorighello 33
Via francesco flores
d'arcais 39
Via francesco maria
colle 33, 41
Via francesco marzolo
14, 15
Via francesco nullo . . 27
Via francesco petrarca
12
Via francesco piccoli . 35
Via francesco rismondo
9, 15, 16
Via francesco robortello
39
Via francesco schubert
9
Via francesco severi . 31,
39
Via francesco squar-
cione 20
Via francesco vannozzo
25
Via fratelli ruffini 14
Via frà giovanni eremi-
tano 5,
6
Via frà paolo sarpi . . 5, 6
Via gabriele d'annunzio
28
Via gabriele falloppio 22,
23
Via gaetano casati 3
Via gaetano giardino 3, 4
Via galileo galilei . 21, 22
Via garigliano 10
Via gaspara stampa . . 21
Via gaspare gozzi . . 7, 14
Via gastone picchini . 27
Via gattamelata . . 23–25,
30, 31, 33
Via generale cantore 35,
36
Via genova 26, 34
Via gentile de filippesi
37
Via gherardo ghirardini
40
Via giacinto carini 3

Via giacomo andrea
giacomini 40
Via giacomo ferretto . 39
Via giacomo leopardi 29,
30, 37, 38
Via giacomo matteotti
12, 13
Via giacomo medici . . . 3
Via giacomo salomonio
39
Via giacomo zanella . . 8
Via giambattista belzoni
22, 23
Via giambattista maga-
nza 37
Via giambattista mor-
gagni 13, 14,
22
Via giambattista verci 32
Via giambattista vico . 36
Via giambellino 17
Via giampaolo vla-
covich 38,
39
Via giannantonio rizzi-
zannoni 3
Via giordano bruno . . 36,
37
Via giordano offreducci
25
Via giosuè carducci . 28,
36
Via giotto 5, 12, 13
Via giovan battista ferro
7
Via giovanni ameglio . . 3
Via giovanni anghinoni
21
Via giovanni battista da
monte 4
Via giovanni battista
ricci 9
Via giovanni battista
tiepolo 23, 24
Via giovanni berchet . 14
Via giovanni bertacchi
40
Via giovanni canestrini
39–41
Via giovanni cittadella 13
Via giovanni da gaibana
6
Via giovanni da nono . 31
Via giovanni de lemizzo
36
Via giovanni gradenigo
15, 16, 24

Via giovanni lazara . . . 31, 32, 40
Via giovanni malaman 36
Via giovanni marcanova 5
Via giovanni marchesini 38, 39
Via giovanni maria fal- conetto 29
Via giovanni omboni . 20
Via giovanni poleni . . . 15
Via giovanni prati 20
Via giovanni storlato . . 7
Via girolamo dal santo 6, 7
Via girolamo frigimelica 19
Via girolamo orlandini . 9
Via giulio alessio . . 13, 14
Via giuseppe cesare abba 3
Via giuseppe dalla ve- dova 5
Via giuseppe ferrari . 29, 37
Via giuseppe gennari . 5
Via giuseppe impastato 8
Via giuseppe jappelli 14, 22
Via giuseppe martucci 9
Via giuseppe orus 24
Via giuseppe peano . . . 3
Via giuseppe perin . . 39, 40
Via giuseppe toniolo . 33
Via giuseppe vaccari 3, 4
Via giuseppe verdi . . . 12
Via giuseppe veronese 30, 38
Via giustiniani 23
Via goffredo mameli . . 6
Via goito 26, 34, 35
Via gorizia 20, 21
Via gregorio ricci- curbastro 31, 39
Via gualchiere 20
Via guglielmino tem- pesta 36
Via guglielmo cortusio 24
Via guglielmo marconi 27, 35
Via guglielmo oberdan 20, 21

Via guglielmo ongarello 40, 41
Via guglielmo pecori giraldi 3
Via guido puchetti 17
Via guisto de menaboui 7
Via gustavo de leva . . 31
Via gustavo modena 30, 31
Via gustavo tartini 30, 31
Via inigo campioni 9
Via ippolito taine 32
Via isabella andreini . 20
Via isabella ravignana 30
Via isidoro wiel 11
Via ivo scapolo . . . 36, 37
Via ivrea 26
Via jacopo avanzo . . 6–9
Via jacopo bonfadini . 39
Via jacopo cavacio . . 33, 40
Via jacopo corrado . . . 25
Via jacopo crescini . . 37– 39
Via jacopo da montag- nana 7, 8
Via jacopo da verona . . 9
Via jacopo facciolati . 30, 31, 39, 40
Via jacopo filiasi . . 33, 41
Via jacopo filippo tom- masini 40
Via jacopo stellini 29, 30
Via jacopo stretto 37
Via l'aquila 34
Via lazzaro bonamico 30
Via leonardo emo- capodilista 36
Via leonardo loredan 14, 15
Via leopoldo ferri 30
Via lepanto 18
Via levi-civita 31
Via livorno 26, 34
Via lodovico barbo . . . 32
Via lorenzo perosi 9
Via lorenzo pignoria . 40
Via loreto 34
Via lovarini 31, 38
Via lovato lovati 25
Via lucindo faggin 6
Via ludovico antonio muratori 4
Via ludovico ariosto . . 17, 25

Via ludovico bressan . . 7
Via luigi anelli 17
Via luigi bottazzo . 30, 38
Via luigi cadorna . 27, 28, 35
Via luigi carlo farini . 7, 14
Via luigi cherubini 7
Via luigi configliachi . . 28
Via luigi duse 23, 31
Via luigi lucatello . 13, 14
Via luigi luzzatti . . . 14, 15
Via luigi mascherpa . . . 9
Via luigi negrelli 18
Via luigi padrin 31
Via luigi pastro 9
Via luigi pellizzo 25
Via luigi piccinato . 14, 15
Via luigi pulci 25
Via luigi settembrini . . 40
Via madonnetta 20
Via malta 6
Via marcel proust 32, 40
Via marchetto da padova 37, 38
Via marco antonio calza 24
Via marco guazzo 33
Via marco mantua be- navides 39
Via marco polo . . . 35, 36
Via marghera 36
Via marsala 20
Via marsilio da padova 12, 20
Via martiri della libertà 12, 13
Via marzolo 15
Via medici 24, 32
Via melchiorre cesarotti 21, 22
Via mentana 18, 26
Via michelangelo buonarroti 6
Via michele montaigne 32, 33, 40
Via michele sanmicheli 29, 30, 36, 37
Via milazzo 18
Via monaco padovano 31, 32
Via monsignor girolamo bortignon 33
Via monte asolone . . . 18
Via monte cimone . . . 10
Via monte di pietà . . . 20
Via monte grappa 18
Via monte nero 18

Via monte ortigara . . . 18
Via monte pasubio . . . 18
Via monte pertica 34
Via monte sabotino . . 18
Via monte solarolo . . . 18
Via monte suello 10
Via montebello . . . 18, 26
Via montello 18
Via monterotondo 10
Via montona 12
Via montà 3
Via nancy 14
Via narni 34
Via nazareth 31, 32
Via nazario sauro . 12, 20
Via niccolò ormaneto 24,
    25
Via niccolò tommaseo 6,
    7, 14–16
Via nicolò copernico . 37
Via nicolò giustiniani . 23,
    31
Via nicolò orsini . . . 10, 18
Via nino bixio 6
Via novara 26
Via ognibene della
    scola 40
Via ognissanti 23, 24
Via oliviero ronchi 40
Via oreste da molin . . . 8
Via oreste ravanello . . 36
Via orto botanico 29
Via ospedale civile . . . 22
Via otello renato pighin
    27
Via padre placido
    cortese 9
Via padre reginaldo giu-
    liani 10
Via palermo . . . 26, 34, 35
Via palestro 18
Via paolo camillo thaon
    di revel 27, 28
Via paolo paruta . 38, 39
Via paolotti 14, 22
Via pasquale paoli . . . 27
Via patriarcato . 11, 19, 20
Via pavia 26
Via perugia 34
Via piave 10, 18
Via pier andrea sac-
    cardo 29
Via pier paolo vergerio
    30, 31, 38
Via pietro arduino 38
Via pietro balan . . . 37, 38

Via pietro barozzi 24, 25,
    32
Via pietro brandolese 40
Via pietro calzetta 6
Via pietro canal 4, 11
Via pietro ceoldo 32
Via pietro d'abano 12, 20
Via pietro de silvestri . 27
Via pietro fortunato
    calvi 13
Via pietro liberi 6, 7
Via pietro maroncelli 16,
    17
Via pietro scalcerle . . 30
Via pietro selvatico . . 7, 8
Via pilade bronzetti . 3, 4,
    10
Via pileo da prata . 25, 33
Via pio chicchi 30, 31
Via pompeo molmenti
    32
Via ponte molino 12
Via ponte ognissanti . 24,
    25
Via porciglia . . . 11–16, 19,
    23, 24, 27, 35
Via pordenone 6
Via premuda 3, 4
Via prosdocimo beldo-
    mandi 4,
    5
Via quarto 3, 10
Via raggio di sole 3, 4, 10
Via ravenna 26, 34
Via redipuglia 16
Via rialto 20
Via riccardo drigo 7
Via riccardo wagner . . . 9
Via rimini 26
Via rinaldo rinaldi . 21, 22
Via roberto ardigò . . . 38
Via roberto de visiani 38,
    39
Via roberto marin 28
Via roberto schumann 9
Via rolandino 25
Via rolando da piazzola
    12
Via roma 20, 21
Via romolo fowst 5
Via romolo gessi 3
Via rudena 21, 28, 29
Via ruggero leoncavallo
    7
Via s.francesco 22
Via salerno 34, 35
Via san biagio 21, 22

Via san camillo de lellis
    32
Via san canziano . . 20, 21
Via san clemente 20
Via san fermo 12, 13
Via san filippo benizzi 40
Via san francesco . 21, 22
Via san gaetano . . 14, 22
Via san giovanni di ver-
    dara 4, 5,
    11
Via san girolamo 20
Via san gregorio bar-
    barigo 20
Via san leonardo muri-
    aldo 15,
    16
Via san martino e
    solferino 20, 21
Via san massimo . 23, 24
Via san mattia 22
Via san nicolò 12
Via san pietro . . 11, 12, 19
Via san pio x 27, 35
Via san polo 12
Via san prosdocimo . 18,
    19
Via san roberto bel-
    larmino 39
Via san siro 39
Via san tomaso 19
Via sandro godina 9
Via sant'agnese 12
Via sant'alberto magno
    27
Via sant'andrea 12, 13, 21
Via sant'eufemia . 22, 23
Via sant'osvaldo 39
Via santa caterina . . . 22
Via santa chiara 21
Via santa lucia . 12, 13, 20
Via santa maria in conio
    15, 23
Via santa maria in vanzo
    27, 35, 36
Via santa rita 31, 39
Via santa rosa 19, 20
Via santa sofia 21, 22
Via sanudo marin 32
Via saverio mercadante
    7
Via savona 26, 34
Via sebastiano gia-
    comelli 39
Via sebastiano melan 39
Via sertorio orsato . . . 31
Via simone stratico . . . 15

Via siracusa 34, 35
Via sondrio 34
Via sorio 18
Via sotto il salone 20
Via sperone speroni . . 19
Via stefano badoer . . . 37
Via stefano canzio 3
Via stefano dall'arzere 6,
    7
Via stefano gallini 32
Via stefano turr 3
Via stefano venturato 33,
    41
Via stendhal 32, 33
Via suor elisabetta ven-
    dramini 5,
    12
Via teobaldo ciconi . . 10,
    11
Via teofilo folengo 18, 19,
    27
Via teofilo gautier . 32, 33
Via tirana 10
Via tito vanzetti 15
Via tiziano aspetti 6
Via todesco 38
Via tommaseo 15
Via tommaso antonio
    catullo 37, 38
Via torino 26
Via torquato tasso 12
Via trasea 24
Via tre garofani 36
Via trieste 5, 13–15
Via tripoli 18
Via tunisi 5
Via ugo bassi 15
Via ugo fernandi 3
Via ugo foscolo 6, 7
Via uguccio de boso . 37
Via umberto cagni 3
Via umberto i 20, 28
Via urbino 34

Via valerio flacco . . 17, 25
Via vecchio gasometro
    13, 14
Via venezia 15–17
Via vercelli 26
Via vicenza 10
Via viii febbraio 21
Via vincenzo de vit . . . 41
Via vincenzo gallucci 22
Via vincenzo stefano
    breda 12, 20
Via vittoria aganoor . . 29,
    30
Via vittorino zanibon . 10
Via vittorio emanuele ii
    28, 36
Via vittorio lazzarini . . 39
Via vittorio polacco . . 40
Via volturno 10, 18
Via zabarella 21
Via zambon de' dauli . . 4
Viale codalunga . 5, 6, 12
Viale della pace 6–8
Viale della rotonda 5
Viale felice cavallotti 35,
    36
Viale giorgio perlasca 13
Viale lanfranco zancan
    4, 5
Vicolo bernardo par-
    entino 6
Vicolo brigata abruzzi 10
Vicolo cappellato pe-
    drocchi 21
Vicolo castelfidardo . . 26
Vicolo cigolo 28
Vicolo dei conti 20
Vicolo dei dotto 12
Vicolo dei servi 20
Vicolo del livello 11
Vicolo del portello 15, 16
Vicolo dell'osservatorio
    19, 27

Vicolo della bovetta . . 12
Vicolo delle camelie . 36
Vicolo delle ortensie 36,
    37
Vicolo delle verbene 36
Vicolo fortebracci 23
Vicolo giovanni battista
    tiepolo 23
Vicolo giovanni
    brunacci 5
Vicolo giuseppe mazz-
    ini 5
Vicolo giuseppe perin
    39, 40
Vicolo michelangelo
    bonarroti 6
Vicolo odasi tifi . . . 39, 40
Vicolo ognissanti . 23, 24
Vicolo pastori 24
Vicolo ponte molino . . 12
Vicolo pontecorvo . . . 30
Vicolo san benedetto 11
Vicolo san massimo . . 23
Vicolo sant'andrea . . . 21
Vicolo santa margherita
    21
Vicolo santa maria in
    conio 15, 23
Vicolo santonini . . 29, 30
Vicolo selvatico es-
    tense 19
Vicolo tabacco . . . 28, 29
Vicolo tiziano aspetti . . 6
Vicolo usuelli 30
Vicolo vincenzo bellini
    14
Vicolo vincenzo gaz-
    zotto 7
Volto del salone 20
Volto dell'orologio . . . 20
Volto della corda 20

Points of Interest

A

Abbey of Santa Giustina (Via G.Ferrari 2) 👤 29
Antenor's Tomb (Piazza Antenore) 👤 21
Art Museum-Palazzo Zabarella (Via Zarabella 14) 🏛 21
Autostazione-Bus Station 🚌 6, 7

B

Basilica Sant'Antonio (Piazza del Santo) 👤 29
Bastion Alicorno 👤 . . . 35
Botanical Garden 👤 . . 29
Botanical Garden Santa Giustina 👤 37
Bridge and Gate Molino 👤 12
Bridge San Leonardo 👤 12

C

Carabinieri HQ 🚓 16
Carabinieri Police Station 🚓 28
Casa Bonandini 👤 . . . 20
Castello Carrarese 👤 19, 27
Church and Cultural Center Altinate San Gaetano 🏛 14
Church and Museum of the Eremitani 🏛 . 13

Church and Museum San Tomaso (Via S.Tomaso 4) 👤 . . . 19
Church Beata Vergine Maria Immacolata 👤 23
Church Cristo Re 👤 . . 39
Church delle Pace 👤 . . 7
Church Holy Spirit 👤 . 33
Church Madonna Addolorata al Torresino (Via A.Memmo 27) 👤 28
Church Nativita 👤 3
Church Ognissanti 👤 . 24
Church Sacra Famiglia 👤 26
Church San Camillio 👤 32
Church San Nicolò 👤 . 12
Church San Paolo 👤 . 40
Church San Pietro 👤 . 11
Church San Pio X 👤 . . 17
Church Santa Croce (Via V.Emanuele II 166) 👤 36
Church Santa Maria dei Servi (Via Roma) 👤 20
Church Santa Maria in Vanzo (Via A.Cavalletto) 👤 28
Church Santa Rita 👤 . 38
Church Santa Sofia 👤 22
Church St.Andrew the Apostle (Via Sant'Adrea) 👤 . . . 13
Church St.Benedetto 👤 11
Church St.Prosdocimo 👤 30
Convent San Francisco

(Via S.Francesco 118) 👤 21
Crystal Garden 👤 . 16, 17

D

Duomo-Cathedral and Diocesan Museum 🏛 20

E

Exhibition Center PadovaFiere 👤 8, 15

F

Forcellini 🏢 33

G

Gym Walter Petron 🤾 23

H

Historic Caffè Pedrocchi XVIII sec. 👤 21
Hospital Associazione La Nostra Famiglia (Via G.Carducci 25) ✚ 36
Hospital Azienda Ospedaliera ✚ . 22, 23, 30, 31
Hospital Sant'Antonio ✚ 39

L

Local Police Station 🚓 6

Loggia Amulea (Prato della Valle 102) 👤 28

Loggia Carrarese (Via Accademia 3) 👤 .20

Loggia del Gran Guardia 👤 20

Loggia e Odeo Cornaro 👤 22

M

Military Hospital ✚ . . 4, 5

Monument Equestre al Gattamelata (Piazza del Santo) 👤 29

Monument Memoria e Luce 👤 13

Museum al Santo (Piazza del Santo 12) 🏛 29

Museum of Astronomy 🏛 19

Museum of Geography (Via del Santo 26) 🏛 21

Museum of History of Medicine 🏛 21

Museum of Minerology 🏛 13

Museum of Paleontology 🏛 13

Museum of Pathology (Via A.Cabelli 59) 🏛 22

Museum of the History of Physics 🏛 14

Museum of thhe Astronomical Observatory-La Specola 🏛 27

Museum of Zoology (Via G.Jappelli 1) 🏛 14

Museum Third Army (Via Altinate 59) 🏛 13

Music Conservatorium Cesare Pollini 🏛 . 13

Music Conservatory Cesare Pollini - succursale bertacchi 🏛 40

MUSME-Science Museum (Via S.Francesco 94) 👤 21

O

Oratory San Michele 👤 27

Oratory San Rocco 🏛 12

Oratory St.Giorgio (Piazza del Santo) 👤 29

P

Padova Train Station 🚆 6, 7

Palazzo Cavalli (Via Vescovado 86) 👤 19

Palazzo del Capitaniato 🏛 20

Palazzo del Monte di Pietà (Piazza Duomo 14) 👤 20

Palazzo della Ragione 👤 20

Palazzo Luzzato 🏛 . . . 19

Palazzo Maldura-Faculty of Humanities 🏛 12

Palazzo Moroni-Commune di Padua 👤 21

Palazzo Zuckermann-Art Museum Bottacin and Museum of Applied Arts (Corso G.Garibaldi) 🏛 . . . 13

Parish Santa Maria del Carmine (Via del Carmine) 👤 12

Piazza Cavour 👤 . . 13, 21

Piazza dei Fruti 👤 20

Piazza Prato della Valle 👤 28, 29

Planetarium 👤 24

Porta Altinate (Piazza G.Garibaldi) 👤 . . . 13

Porta Ognissanti 👤 . . . 15

Porta Pontecorvo 👤 . 30

Porta Savonarola 👤 . . 10

Prefecture of Padua👤 21

S

Sacra Famiglia 🏢 34

Sant'Osvaldo 🏢 40

Santuary San Leopoldo Mandic 👤 35

Scrovegni Chapel in Garden Arena 👤 . 13

Seminary Maggiore 🏛 28

Skating Ring ⛸ 37

Soccer Field San Paolo ⛸ 40, 41

Sports Complex Arcella ⛸ 7, 8

Sports Complex Sacra Famiglia (Via Perugia 3) ⛸ 34

Stadium Silvio Appiani ⛸ 36

Stanga 🏢 23

T

Theatre G.Verdi 👤 12

Torre dell'Orologio (Piazza dei Signori) 👤 20

Torrione della Gatta and Rotonda Gardens 👤 5

Torrione di santa giustina 👤 37

Tourist Office 🛈 6

Traffic Police 🚓 37

U

University Hospital Giustinianeo ✚ 22, 23

University of Padua 🏛 14–16, 19, 22, 24

University of Padua-Palazzo Bo 👤 21

V

Villa Canale 👤 28

Villa Montesi 👤 35

Villa Tron 👤 29

Made in the USA
Las Vegas, NV
15 August 2024

93861836R00031